BOOK 2

Learning to Play

FOR YOUNG PIANISTS

By **MELVIN STECHER**
NORMAN HOROWITZ
and
CLAIRE GORDON

ISBN 0-7935-5267-2

G. SCHIRMER, *Inc.*

DISTRIBUTED BY

HAL•LEONARD®
CORPORATION
7777 W. BLUEMOUND RD. P.O. BOX 13819 MILWAUKEE, WI 53213

LET'S LOOK AT MUSIC

In Book 1 you have already learned:

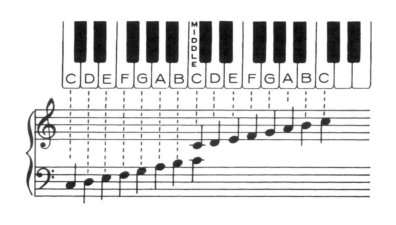

QUARTER NOTE	♩	**1** count
HALF NOTE	♪	**2** counts
DOTTED HALF NOTE	♪.	**3** counts
WHOLE NOTE	o	**4** counts

SHARP ♯   **FLAT** ♭   **NATURAL** ♮

TIE   **STACCATO**

loud **f**   soft **p**

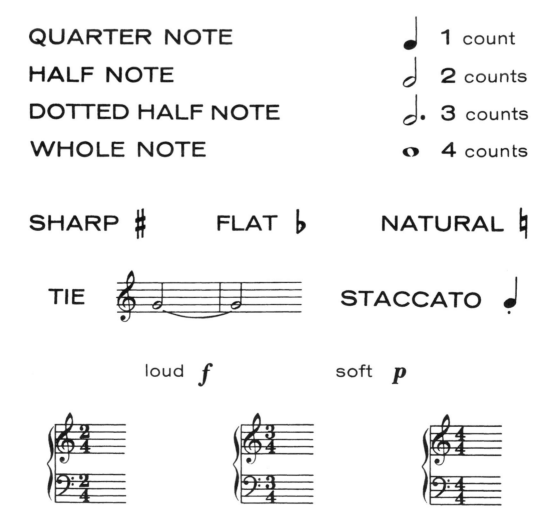

The Trampoline

On a Holiday

The Caravan

Follow the Rainbow

A Sunday Walk

6

RESTS are signs for silence and
are counted the same as notes.

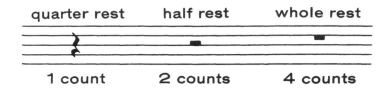

quarter rest	half rest	whole rest
1 count	2 counts	4 counts

Hop, Hop, Hop!

Lively

German

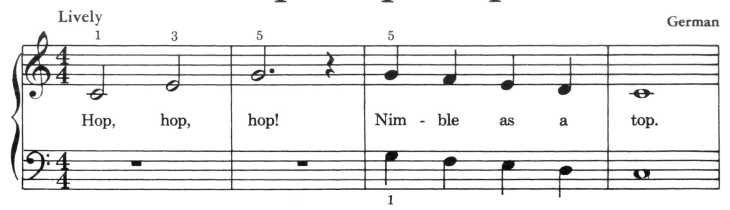

Hop, hop, hop! Nim - ble as a top.

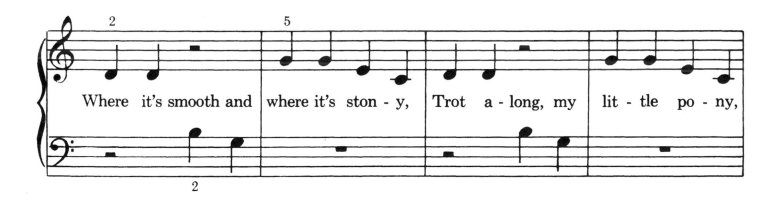

Where it's smooth and where it's ston - y, Trot a - long, my lit - tle po - ny,

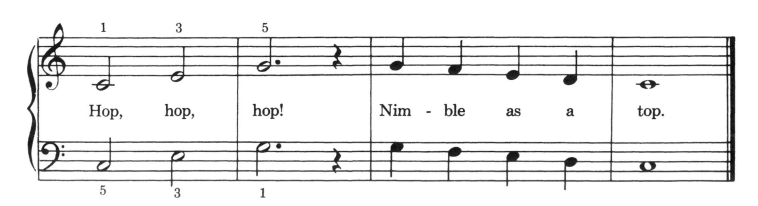

Hop, hop, hop! Nim - ble as a top.

There are sentences in language. There are also sentences in music.

A sentence in music is called a **PHRASE.**

Play the notes in each phrase **LEGATO** (smoothly)

and make a little break between phrases.

The Rocking Chair

Ten Little Indians

TEACHER

American

These are **EIGHTH NOTES** ♪♪

They can also be written like this ♫

Two eighth notes are counted in the time of one quarter note.

♫ = ♩

Ten Little Indians

PUPIL

American

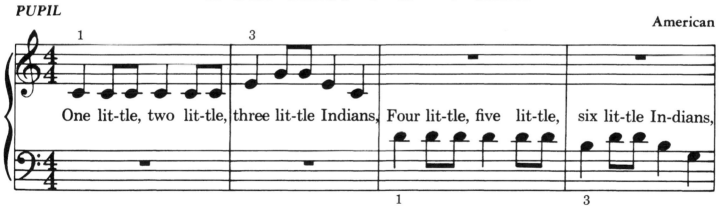

One lit-tle, two lit-tle, three lit-tle Indians, Four lit-tle, five lit-tle, six lit-tle In-dians,

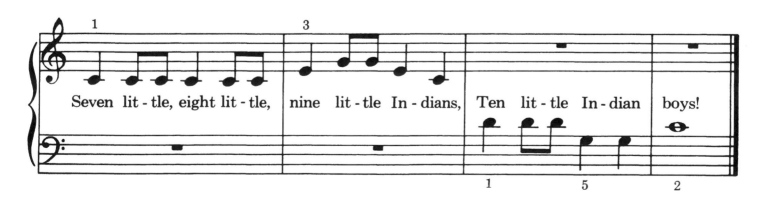

Seven lit-tle, eight lit-tle, nine lit-tle In-dians, Ten lit-tle In-dian boys!

Skip to My Lou

TEACHER

American

Skip to My Lou

American

PUPIL

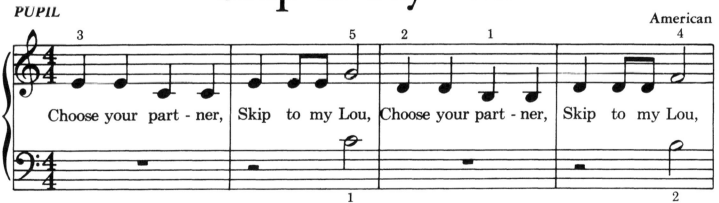

Choose your part - ner, Skip to my Lou, Choose your part - ner, Skip to my Lou,

Choose your part - ner, Skip to my Lou, Skip to my Lou, my dar - ling!

At the Toy Shop

CRESCENDO means gradually louder.

DIMINUENDO means gradually softer.

The Shoemaker

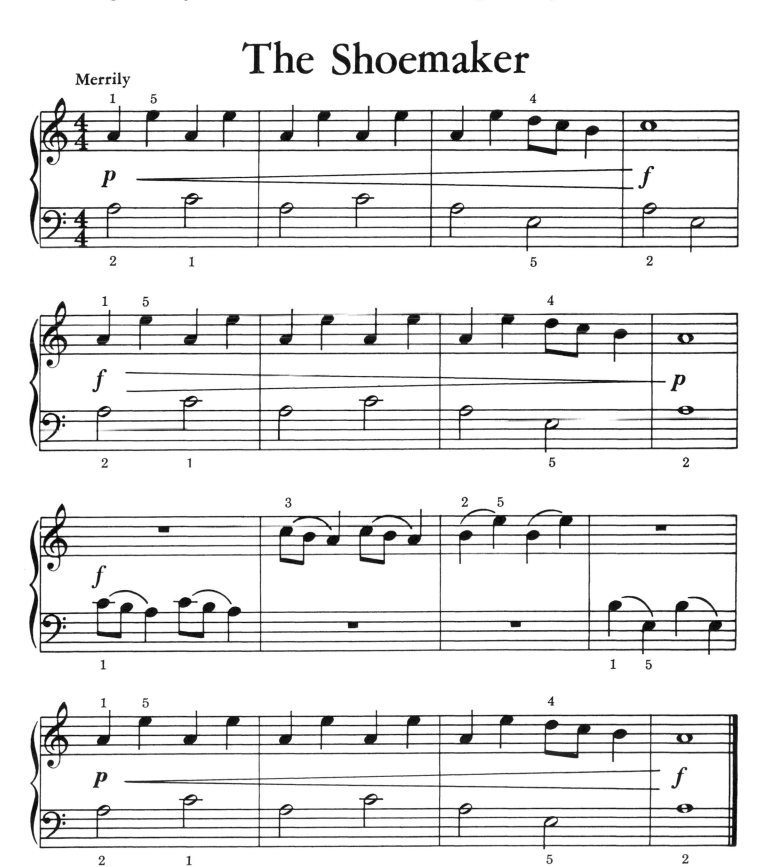

A **MAJOR SCALE** has eight tones.
It is made up of whole steps and half steps.

A **HALF STEP** is the distance from any key
to the very next key, black or white,
in either direction.

A **WHOLE STEP** is the distance of two half steps.

The whole and half steps in a major
scale are always in the same order.

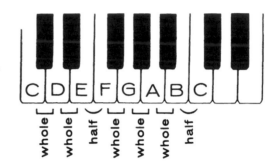

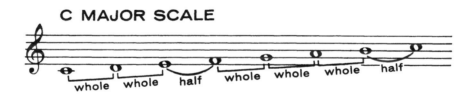

A major scale can be built on any tone.
Using the pattern of whole steps and half steps,
the major scale starting on G always has an f-sharp.

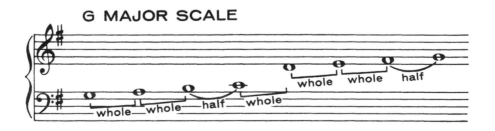

The **KEY SIGNATURE** of G major is one sharp.

The sharp on the f line after each clef

reminds us always to play f–sharp.

This piece is in the **KEY** of G.

Riding the Ferryboat

Gently and flowing

16

The distance from one note to another note is called an **INTERVAL**.

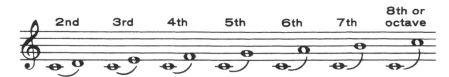

The Pogo Stick

With marked rhythm

Country Dance

Sweet Betsy from Pike

TEACHER

American

Sweet Betsy from Pike

PUPIL

American

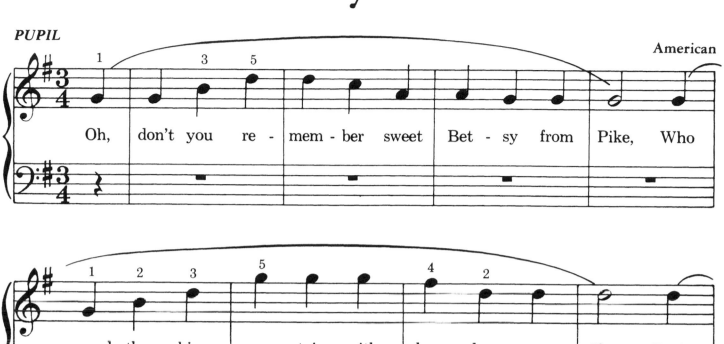

Oh, don't you re - mem - ber sweet Bet - sy from Pike, Who

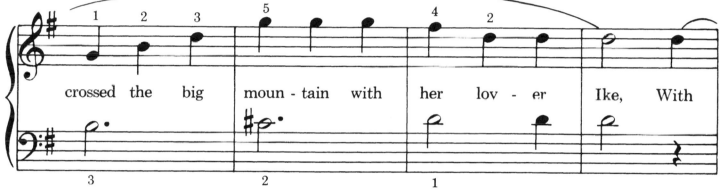

crossed the big moun - tain with her lov - er Ike, With

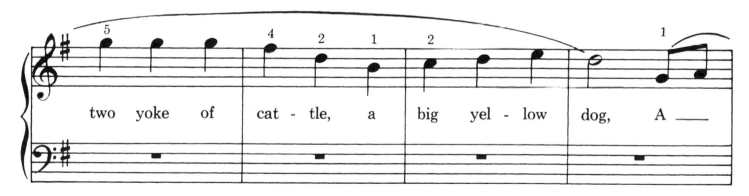

two yoke of cat - tle, a big yel - low dog, A ____

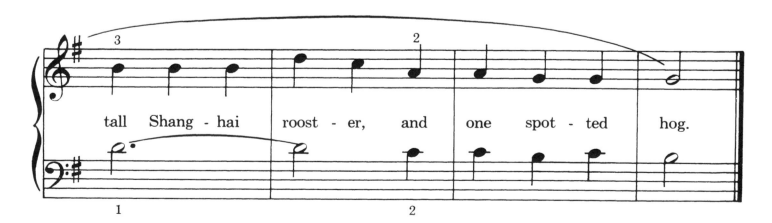

tall Shang - hai roost - er, and one spot - ted hog.

20

The key signature of F major is one flat.
The flat on the b line after each clef
reminds us always to play b-flat.
This piece is in the key of F.

Scouts on Parade

In march time

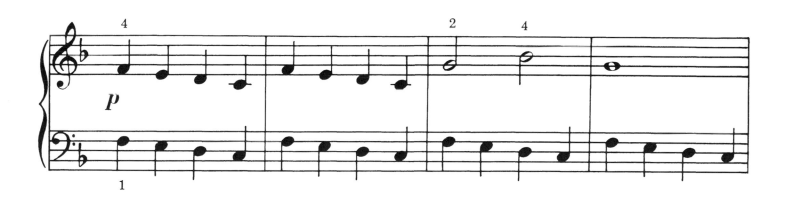

22

This is a **DOTTED QUARTER NOTE** 𝅘𝅥𝅭
It is counted the same as a quarter note tied to an eighth note.

Alouette

French-Canadian

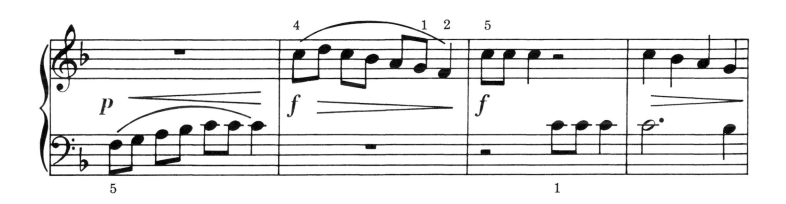

This is an **EIGHTH REST** 𝄾

It is counted the same as an eighth note.

The King's Palace

24

This is an **ACCENT** >
An accent above or below a note
means to play that note louder
than the other notes.

Baby Elephant

With marked rhythm

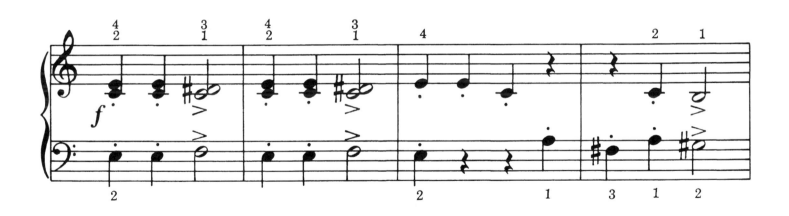

RITARDANDO means gradually slower.

Falling Leaves

In SIX-EIGHT TIME

there are six counts in each measure and each eighth note gets one count.

Three Blind Mice

Traditional

The Acrobat

With excitement

The Waterfall

Bagpipers